Christmas Inspirations

Book 1

8 Intermediate to Late Intermediate Seasonal Piano Arrangements that Motivate & Entertain

George Peter Tingley

As a professional pianist, I always look forward to performing during the winter holiday season. There is something about Christmas that brings out the best in my playing. As a teacher, composer and arranger, I always strive to put into the hands of my students those very sounds that have worked so well in performance. Christmas Inspirations is a collection of seasonal favorites in arrangements that draw upon such sounds: warm and lush harmonies, classical textures, ragtime rhythms—even some country piano stylings. Pianists are sure to find these impressive arrangements a joy to practice as well as perform.

George Peter Tingley

Cover photo: © John Lawrence/Tony Stone Images

O Come, All Ye Faithful

J. F. Wade
Arr. by George Peter Tingley

Gently

13
pp subito
cresc.
16
mf
pp
p
19
mp
cresc.
22
f
dim. e riten.
a tempo
8va
p
25
(8va)
dim. e rall.
pp

God Rest Ye Merry, Gentlemen

Traditional English Carol
Arr. by George Peter Tingley

16
fp
19
p
cresc.
22
fp
mp
legato ed espressivo
26
mf
dim. e rit.
29
a tempo
p
pp
mp
dim. e rit.
Slow
pp
8va
ppp

Up on the Housetop

B. R. Handby
Arr. by George Peter Tingley

Cheerful

17
mp
21
mf
mp
25
mf
29

33
mf
mp
36
cresc.
40
f
mf
43
pp
mf
f

It Came Upon the Midnight Clear

Richard S. Willis
Arr. by George Peter Tingley

17
21
p
f
25
29
mp
rall. e dim.
LH
pp
a tempo
p
simile

33
37
mf
mp
riten.
simile
41
a tempo
p
45
mp
rall. e dim.
LH
pp
a tempo
p
RH
LH
dim. e rit.
RH
pp

Deck the Halls

Welsh Carol
Arr. by George Peter Tingley

12
riten.
a tempo
mf
p
15
mp
p
18
cresc.
21
mf
f
riten.
24
a tempo
mp
p
rall.
pp

Jingle Bells

James Pierpont
Arr. by George Peter Tingley

18
mp
22
mf
26
mp
30
34
mf

38
42
p
fp
fp
46
mf
allargando
Slower than before
51
f

55
59
f
8va
(loco)
63
8va
cresc.
67
(8va)
ff
dim.
RH
mp
8va
sfz
8va

Joy to the World

George Friedrich Handel
Arr. by George Peter Tingley

13
p
mp
16
f
19
dim.
mp
22
rallentando
Slowly
p
RH
LH
RH

Silent Night

Franz Grüber
Arr. by George Peter Tingley

17
p
21
25
mp
mf
29
mp
rallen.
a tempo
p
mp

33
mf
simile
37
41
mp
45
p

49
mp
cresc.
f
53
mp
simile
p
57
a tempo
mf
rallen.
p
61
pp
rit.

Alfred